Perspectives

Uncontacted People
Should We Leave Them Alone?

Flying Start
to Literacy®

Contents

Introduction

How do we help uncontacted people?

There are groups of people that live in isolated places: deep in thick jungles, on remote islands or high in dense mountainous regions. They have no interaction with the outside world. And that's how they like it! They are called uncontacted people.

Some people believe we should contact remote tribes and provide them with medical help, food, tools, and other supplies and information. Other people say we should not contact them; we should leave them in peace! And some people don't want to help them at all – they want to use the land where remote tribes live to mine for gold, log trees or build farms.

Is there a way to help uncontacted people? Do they need help?

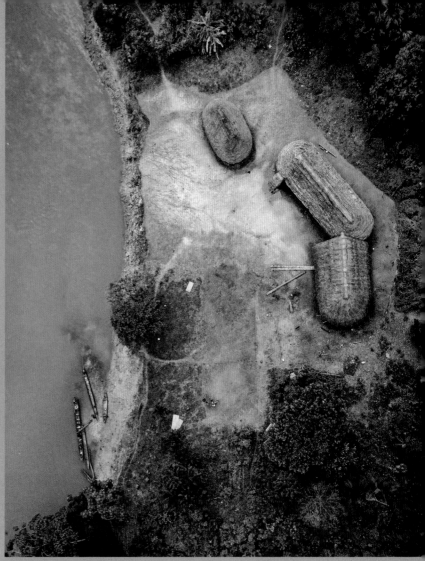

5

Stay away!

There are about 100 groups of native people who live in isolated places and have no contact with the outside world. And they do not want to make contact.

In this article, Joshua Hatch presents some very persuasive arguments for leaving these people alone. Does he succeed in persuading you? What is your opinion?

Don't make contact!

Uncontacted people live in places that are difficult to access, often far from cities, towns and villages. These tribes should not be contacted by outsiders.

Some of these people live on remote islands, or hidden in hard-to-reach areas of the jungle. They might see planes flying overhead or hear the sounds of machines in the distance, but these people do not interact with what many refer to as the modern world.

Instead, they live off the land and have their own unique languages and cultures. Still, some people want to visit them. They want to convert the tribes to a different religion. Or they want to convince the tribes to leave their land so it can be mined or farmed.

The San of Namibia are the indigenous people of southern Africa. Their ancestors have lived in this region for tens of thousands of years.

But making contact is not a good idea. When people connect with isolated native people, bad things happen – usually to the native people.

For example, an uncontacted tribe called the Jarawa that lived on an island off the coast of India hadn't made contact with the outside world for 30,000 to 50,000 years. In 1999, however, an outside group arrived. And when it did, the outsiders passed on their germs – spreading colds, the flu, measles and other illnesses – and many native people got sick and died.

Unfortunately, that's typical. Most uncontacted people have never been exposed to the modern world's diseases. They lack immunities, so they are susceptible to getting sick.

The people who visited the Jarawa weren't trying to hurt them, but that's not always the case with other groups that want to make contact.

The Jarawa people catch crabs and fish in
the coral reefs surrounding their island.

Illegal logging in the Amazon rainforest, Peru

Manu National Park, Peru, home to the Mashco-Piro people

In Peru, some people want to cut down ancient trees in an area where a tribe called the Mashco-Piro live. This tribe has lived in isolation for many years, but the loggers don't care. They want to cut down the trees and sell the lumber.

Obviously, that's bad for the Mashco-Piro people, but it's also bad for others, too. Often, these old tribes know how to care for their environment. And if they are gone, nobody will be left to conserve the land. Loggers, miners and others could come in and destroy it all.

When contact results in the destruction of a native people – or it forces the native people to assimilate with the modern population – it can also mean the end of that people's culture, including its language. When you lose your language, you lose your culture.

Most of the time, uncontacted people are isolated for a reason: they want to be left alone. Shouldn't they be granted that? I think so! Especially because outsiders' contact usually harms them.

Lending a hand

Around the world, the population of remote tribes is getting smaller every year. We are at risk of losing the cultures, languages and incredible diversity these people represent.

If we want to prevent those losses from happening, argues Nancy O'Connor, we need to make contact. We can't just watch these tribes get smaller and smaller and eventually die out.

As you read Nancy's article, think about whether we can help them without harming them.

We need to make contact!

Scientists who study the people and cultures of the world are called anthropologists. Most anthropologists argue that uncontacted people deserve to be left alone and that we must respect their right to live their lives in peace – much as they have for thousands of years.

But some anthropologists feel our modern society has a responsibility to reach out to these hidden tribes and offer them help in the safest and most ethical ways possible.

Many of these uncontacted tribes have had bad experiences with outsiders. People like the Piraha tribe in the Amazon rainforest are afraid of outsiders because of the terrible treatment inflicted on them in the past. Remote tribes have been captured, enslaved, struck down by disease and even killed. It is no wonder these people are fearful of strangers.

Today, the tribes face a serious threat from individuals who want their land and feel the indigenous people are in the way of progress. Illegal mining and logging businesses see the land as valuable enough to justify stealing or murder. In other cases, local governments may make plans to dam up rivers without considering that a tribe's homeland could be flooded.

In the past, explorers have accidentally come across some of these Amazon people and been surprised to find that they owned metal pots, pans and tools. They believe these items might have been traded with other nearby tribes that are in closer contact with the modern world. Some anthropologists think that by making contact with these isolated people and offering them similar items – as well as metal spearheads, knives and farming tools – it would make their lives easier.

A bushfire in the Amazon rainforest

Trees in the Amazon rainforest are cleared for mining.

Although these tribes have their own remedies, they could benefit from advances in modern medicine. Many of the illnesses and injuries tribespeople experience could be prevented or cured by today's vaccines and surgical techniques. A child bitten by a jaguar might die from infection. A man who broke his leg falling from a tree might be crippled for life. But today's medical advances could save them from death or injury, and maybe even help keep a tribe from dying out.

Ensuring the well-being of isolated tribes in times of natural disasters is also a valid reason for contact. Volcanic eruptions, earthquakes, bushfires, tsunamis and other catastrophes could completely wipe out a group of people, and the rest of the world might never even know. First responders, doctors and scientists could offer much-needed assistance.

These tribes deserve our help. But can we help them without destroying their way of life?

We can see you!

People in a remote, uncontacted group have noticed something flying overhead.

Ask yourself: What might these people be thinking? How might they be feeling? Why might they feel this way?

The last of his tribe

The number of uncontacted people in our world today is fewer and fewer, and deciding the best way to help them can be a dilemma. The man in this article by Christina Graf is the last surviving member of his tribe, and he will eventually die alone.

Should he be left alone in peace? Under what circumstances would you make contact with him?

The Man of the Hole

A man has lived alone in Brazil's Amazon jungle for more than 25 years. The other five remaining members of his tribe were killed in 1995. No one knows the name of the tribe, how large it was or what happened to its other members.

Many of Brazil's indigenous people have been killed by farmers, loggers or other land-grabbers. As a result, many tribes have retreated deep into the jungle and avoided contact with outsiders. It is believed that more than 100 uncontacted tribes live in the Brazilian Amazon jungle.

FUNAI expedition into the Amazon

The man who lives alone has no contact with the outside world and no one knows what language he speaks. He is monitored by a group in Brazil called FUNAI, or the National Indian Foundation. It is responsible for protecting and monitoring indigenous people.

FUNAI workers made several attempts to make contact with him after they first learnt of his existence. They were concerned about his ability to survive on his own, but he made it clear that he did not want to be contacted – he once fired an arrow at some of the workers, but no one was seriously injured.

The group has since stopped its efforts to contact the man. Its officials continue to monitor him to ensure he remains safe from land-grabbers. The land he lives on has been designated as a protected area.

The man makes small huts out of palm leaves. Inside each hut, he digs a deep rectangular hole in the ground. No one is sure why he digs these holes, but this is why he is called the Man of the Hole.

Gourd

Manioc

Pawpaw

The man carves his own arrowheads and makes water containers out of gourds from the calabash tree. He also uses resin, a sticky substance obtained from trees and plants, to make torches.

He hunts for animals using traps and a bow and arrow. He chops down palm trees with an axe to harvest hearts of palm, the edible core of the trees. He also grows some of his food, including corn and manioc (an edible plant). In addition, he eats honey he harvests from hollow tree trunks, and the nuts and pawpaws he gathers. FUNAI workers leave seeds and tools to help him grow crops.

Outsiders are amazed that the man has survived on his own for so long. FUNAI representative Altair Algayer says: *This man, unknown to us, even losing everything, like his people and a series of cultural practices, has proved that, even then, alone in the middle of the bush, it is possible to survive and resist allying with society.*

The Sentinelese: Keep out!

When an American tried to visit a remote island off the coast of India, he was killed by the islanders.

Why did this happen? Whose fault was it? Why is it important to legally protect these people?

In this article, Kerrie Shanahan explains that the answers to these questions may not be as simple as it first appears.

In 2018, an American man was shot by arrows when he decided to illegally visit a remote island in the Bay of Bengal near India. The man died when the islanders fired the arrows at him.

Laws are in place to protect these people and the young man knew this. He also knew of the dangers. On a previous attempt to visit the island, he was shot at by the islanders and quickly retreated. When he decided to attempt another visit, he knew he was risking his life.

This photo was taken from an aeroplane flying over North Sentinel Island, a remote island off the coast of India.

North Sentinel Island

The islanders are a group of uncontacted people called the Sentinelese and they are one of the most isolated groups in the world. It is difficult to know exactly how many people live on North Sentinel Island. It could be as few as 50 or as many as 400.

They have lived alone on North Sentinel Island for an estimated 60,000 years. Images from drones flying over the island show no evidence of farming, so the islanders probably get their food by hunting and gathering.

The drone images also show the Sentinelese using boats they have made to fish in shallow waters. And they use bits of metal and other materials that have been washed ashore from shipwrecks.

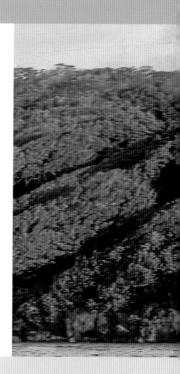

"Visitors" are a threat to the Sentinelese and they aggressively defend their land. People who have tried to come ashore have been shot at with arrows and spears.

After one horrific tsunami, a helicopter with supplies flew overhead to offer help, but a Sentinelese man vigorously fired arrows at it.

The Sentinelese are survivors and they don't want visitors!

The Sentinelese use spears to catch fish and crabs.

What is your opinion? How to write a persuasive argument

1. State your opinion

Think about the issues related to your topic. What is your opinion?

2. Research

Research the information you need to support your opinion.

Related *Perspectives* book   Internet   Other sources

3. Make a plan

Introduction

How will you "hook" the reader?

State your opinion.

List reasons to support your opinion.

What persuasive devices will you use?

Reason 1
Support your reason
with evidence and details.

Reason 2
Support your reason
with evidence and details.

Reason 3
Support your reason
with evidence and details.

Conclusion

Restate your opinion. Leave your reader with a strong message.

4. Publish

Publish your persuasive argument.

Use visuals to reinforce your opinion.